# PRECIOUS & PLEASANT RICHES

## ENCOURAGEMENT FOR THE HOMESCHOOL PARENT

## KRISTI MENASHE

## TO MY LORD AND SAVIOR, JESUS CHRIST

Thank You for the gift of motherhood. Thank You for teaching me so much about Your grace, Your love, and Your forgiveness through my children. You are the perfect parent and the perfect teacher. Psalm 19:14 is the cry of my heart..."May the words of my mouth and the meditation of my heart be pleasing in Your sight, O Lord, my Rock and my Redeemer." Thank You for Your faithfulness and for not giving up on this work in progress!

## TO MY INCREDIBLE HUSBAND, JOSH

Thank you for doing life with me, for raising these beautiful kids with me, for loving your family well, for providing for us, and for answering the phone when our stinkers need a little talking-to from Dad! Thank you for leading us well, and for being the best dad and principal! You are our hero! I love you so much, and I am forever grateful to God for you. Aside from salvation, you are my greatest gift in this life!

## TO MY FOUR PRECIOUS ARROWS

Bryson, Hudson, Keaton, and Quinn...It is a great privilege and an incredible honor to teach you at home! My utmost desire for each of you is that you love and serve Jesus all your days. I hope and pray that you live for an Audience of One. Use your God-given talents for His glory. I am so proud to be your mom and teacher! Thank you for your endless grace, and for teaching me more than I could ever teach you! I love you with my whole heart!

# INTRODUCTION

When I was nine years old and in the fourth grade, my school held a career fair. We chose the career we were interested in, made posters, got all dressed up, and welcomed guests as we acted the part. I chose to be a teacher. My love for bossing people around never wavered, and when I graduated from high school, I went straight to college to pursue a degree in Child and Adolescent Studies. During college, I worked full-time as a preschool teacher. I always enjoyed teaching younger kids (you know, before the sass and attitude kick in!) and after graduating from college, I got a job as a Kindergarten teacher at the school belonging to the church I grew up in. I taught Kindergarten and first grade for several years before having our first son and I loved every minute. Teaching kids to read, to spell, to write sentences, and to add and subtract brought joy to my life. I loved my students and they loved me. In fact, I am still in close contact with many of my former students and their amazing parents today.

I clearly remember saying, "I will NEVER homeschool!" Well, I think we all know what happens when we say we "will NEVER" do something! Often, we wind up doing that very thing! I love how the Lord works in our lives. Sometimes those things that we can never imagine doing are the exact things He will call us to do. But, I am getting ahead of myself...

In August of 2002, our first son was born. I have been blessed to be able to stay home since. When it was time for Bryson to start Kindergarten, I was so excited to tour Christian schools and decide on the very best one for him. My husband, Josh, and I prayed and talked. We decided on a school about fifteen minutes from our house. Bryson enjoyed three years there (K-2), but also struggled to focus. He would come home after sitting in a desk all day and then homework would take two hours. Bryson would wind up in tears, and I would too. I vividly remember sobbing facedown into my carpet, as I thought about how daunting the future years felt. If second grade homework was taking two hours, how much longer would the upper grades take? Toward the end of that school year, the Lord began to prompt my heart. I felt like He would soon be calling me to homeschool. I mentioned it to my husband a few times and his response was always a "nope." I asked him to pray about it, and in late spring when I broached the subject again, Josh told me that he was on board. The Lord had changed his heart, and we were on the same page. Thus began our plan and path to begin homeschooling.

That fall of 2011, I had two students! Bryson was entering third grade, and our second son, Hudson, was entering Kindergarten. I was so excited to teach my two boys. We transformed one of our bedrooms into a classroom, decorated all of the walls, and bought school desks. We said the Pledge of Allegiance each day, and also pledged to the Christian flag and to the Bible. (It would take me several years to realize that I was trying to copy, model, and adopt many public and private school philosophies, rules, and schedules.) We enjoyed many field trips, got together with other homeschool families for holiday parties, and enjoyed the flexibility that homeschooling brought to our family. We became pregnant with Keaton that first year, and he was born a month into summer. In the summer of 2015, we spent two weeks in China, and brought our adopted daughter, Quinn, home. In all of our ten years, only that first year was "quiet." In our years to follow, we would have a newborn, a toddler, then two toddlers, and eventually a total of four students. At the end of each school year, I am always amazed at how the Lord provides and gets us through!

In 2014, I attended a Christian homeschool convention (shout out to CHEA!) and I left feeling extremely pumped. I was so encouraged after hearing the different speakers and learning new things that I could implement in our school and home. The thing about that particular convention is that it's typically held during summer. If you're a homeschooler- you really love summer and you enjoy NOT having to think about lesson plans and purchasing curriculum for a few months! Am I right? I remember leaving the convention wishing that our church had a homeschool ministry. I attend a very large church (shout out to Calvary Chapel Chino Hills!) and there are many homeschooling families in our body. Over the next several months I prayed, met with my pastor's wife, and was compelled to take the necessary steps to get a ministry up and running.

When we were choosing a name for the ministry, the Lord brought to mind the passage He had given me before the start of my first homeschool year. *Proverbs 24:3-4 says: "Through wisdom a house is built, and by understanding it is established; By knowledge the rooms are filled with all precious and pleasant riches."* Thus, Established became the name for the ministry at CCCH. It has been a blessing to continue to help lead the ministry at church for the past seven years, in hopes of encouraging parents along the way.

Homeschooling isn't for the faint of heart. It's not all rainbows and roses. It is a sacrifice and a constant learning process for us all. There are certainly days I wish I could forget, but the rewards far outweigh the trials. I have gotten to teach three-fourths of my kids to read. We have enjoyed family vacations throughout the year (because we can take our work with us). We pray together after discipline has been necessary. One-on-one teaching and correction can happen. We read history aloud and then google things we read about. We have the flexibility to meet up with friends for "P.E." at the park or for swimming on a hot day. We can sneak out to grab In-N-Out for lunch. Our older two have helped teach concepts to the younger two. The list of blessings goes on!

I'll forever love this quote I heard years ago: "The Lord doesn't call the equipped. He equips the called." When I apply that to homeschooling, a weight is lifted. As my family continues to walk this road, I know that my God will always be faithful to show up! He will give me all that I need for each day. I don't have to worry or fear "how" we will get through each year. I can look back on the past ten years and see His faithful hand. We can do nothing apart from Him, amen? I believe He loves to reveal His power and might to us. As I think back over the years, I am not exactly sure how we survived a few of them! I am in awe of all He has done, and I thank Him for calling my family to this.

This book exists because I hope to encourage you, by sharing little things the Lord has put on my heart. Some of these devotionals were written years ago, to our list of Established subscribers. Some were written yesterday. Some were written for specific months or seasons of the year. I pray that the Lord will use these devotionals, no matter when you happen to read them, to minister to your heart. I truly feel that we ALL need encouragement and support. On the tough days, we need to be able to phone a friend and ask for prayer. On the happy days, we want others to rejoice with us over all that God is doing. When we learn a lesson or two along the way, we want to pass that along to someone who isn't quite as far down the road as we are. When we talk with those who have pioneered us, we want to glean from them. I have added prayers after each devotional, in an attempt to lead you into dialogue with our amazing Teacher! May He shepherd your heart, as you minister to your children's.

My prayer for you is that you will walk confidently in the plan that God has for YOUR family. That you won't give up when you hit a rough patch (because those are sure to come). That you would press on and not grow weary. That you would never feel inadequate or less-than. That you'd find a confidant you can share the ups and downs with. That you would encourage others, as the Lord leads. That you would enjoy learning alongside your children. That you wouldn't compare yourselves or your children to others, as is our human tendency. That you would always feel you can reach out for prayer! My email is: kmenashewrites@gmail.com and I invite you to allow me the privilege of praying for you and your family.

God bless you on your journey! It won't be easy, but it will be worth it! Whether you homeschool for one year or for twenty-five, may Christ be your Guide. Stick close to the Vine and let Him lead. Be encouraged as you raise up arrows for the Kingdom!


In His Service,

Kristi Menashe

"NINE-TENTHS OF EDUCATION
IS ENCOURAGEMENT."

-ANATOLE FRANCE

AN END
IN SIGHT

# AN END IN SIGHT

An End in Sight might seem to be an odd title for a devotional, as we begin a new school year. But here's the thing: Before we start another school year, we should have an idea of what we want our ending to look like. What are our goals for the upcoming year? What are our hopes and aspirations? I will share a few of mine: that my children would know the Lord in a deeper way, that I would be a more loving and devoted mom and teacher, that I will be able to teach my children- not just "head knowledge" but also valuable life lessons, and that most of all, we would end the year having grown- in the Lord, in our knowledge, and in our relationships with one another.

This year is going to be an interesting one for me, as I will have a preschooler, a kindergartener, a sixth grader, and a freshman! We will represent near every schooling bracket. Sometimes just the thought overwhelms me. Then, I remember that I was called to this. I am called to this. The Lord didn't make a mistake when he filled my quiver with these arrows, nor when He laid it upon my heart and my husband's, to school our children in our home. This next year will be our seventh year of homeschooling, and I don't think I will ever be able to say, "We have arrived!" Some years have been about thriving, while we have had several years that I can only describe as surviving. As I mentally prepare for our upcoming school year, I want it to be a year of thriving, of course. Of seeking, learning, growth, and change.

My brother-in-law shared a quote with me a few years back: "To teach is to learn twice." You may have heard me say it before, because I truly love the truth and simplicity of it. The way I see it- I get to learn again, alongside my children. All of those things that I didn't store away in my memory bank as a young student myself, have a chance at sticking this time around!! I get excited to (re)learn important dates in history, elements on the periodic table, geographical locations, and when to use apostrophes. As a mom, it's exciting to watch my children "get" something. I get to teach my kindergartner to read this year, and I will watch my preschooler learn her letters and how to to write her name. I will enjoy preparing my sixth grader for junior high, and I will probably shed even more tears as I watch my oldest enter high school, mentally recounting the years gone by too quickly.

If you're like me, you have some regrets about things you have or haven't done as a parent and teacher. Maybe you're hard on yourself or even condemn yourself from time to time. Quite possibly, you don't give yourself the grace that you give others, and that the Lord gives you.

As you get ready to enter into this school year, my suggestion is that you (and I am speaking to myself here too) find some quiet time with Jesus. Seek Him and ask Him what He wants your ending to look like. Pray and tell Him your fears, your goals, your hopes. He already knows them, before they're even on your tongue...but pour them all out to Him, simply because His Word tells us to. He desires that we seek Him (Matthew 6:33) and draw near to Him (James 4:8). Start your prayers by saying, "If You will it, Lord..." and end them with "Thy will be done!" We want our teaching, our parenting, and our relationships to be reflections of His goodness. If you're inclined to do so, date a piece of paper and write these thoughts and prayers out- so that at the end of the year, you can look back on your start and see how you've finished. It is because of His goodness that we have the privilege of homeschooling. It is by His grace that we have these arrows to raise. I am excited to begin another year...because I have an end in sight. I am praying the same for you.

# HEAR MY PRAYER:

Abba Father, Thank You for the privilege of teaching my children at home. Lord, keep my eyes fixed on You. I don't want to look too far ahead, lest I become overwhelmed, and yet I fully trust that You have a plan and a purpose for my family. I know that I will be able to look back on this time and see Your hand of faithfulness and providence. I want to reflect You in all I do. I want my children to see You in me. May I be a godly example for my kids. May my desires line up with Yours. I want to be in the center of Your will always. Amen.

# THINKING
# BACK

# THINKING BACK

Is it just me, or does summer seem to fly by? By now, you've likely started school or you will be starting soon! As much as I love summer (and hate to see it end), it's nice to get back into those normal, everyday routines that a new school year brings. It's time to think about lesson-planning, sign-ups, curriculum choices, extracurricular activities, and how to get it all done each week! However, as I prepare to begin a new school year, I can tend to feel overwhelmed. Did I order everything I need? How will I be able to teach three different grade levels? How can I meet all of their needs? Am I forgetting something? Have I filled out all of the required paperwork? And the list goes on! (Please tell me I'm not alone!)

I am heading into my eighth year of homeschooling, and when I begin to feel overwhelmed, I often have to tell myself to stop looking ahead. That may sound funny, but I actually have to think back...over the past ten years. I have to shift my focus and remember ALL that the Lord has done in our family. I have to remind myself of His goodness and faithfulness- and how He has gotten us through each year. Honestly, we have had years of "thriving," but a few have just been about "surviving." Through it all: the ups and downs, the good days and the ones I'd like to forget, the triumphs and the trials...I can say, with absolute certainty, that He has called me to teach my children at home. When He reminds me that He is the One who has called me to this I can rest, knowing that I will be able to look back upon my eighth year in the same light. When the enemy's voice threatens to drown out the One who created me and my kids, I can search the Word, find my footing, and step forward in confidence.

I read Galatians 6:9 this morning and was encouraged: *"And let us not grow weary while doing good, for in due season we shall reap if we do not lose heart."* I am praying for each of you- as you begin your first, your eighth, or your fifteenth year. May HIS voice be louder! Be blessed on your homeschooling journey, as You think back on ALL that the Lord has already done in your life and in your home.

# HEAR MY PRAYER:

God, Thank You for all that You have done in my life. Thank You for working in the lives of my children. Thank You for calling me to homeschool. I don't want to move ahead of You, and I don't want to get trapped in fear. I put my complete faith and trust in You, God. I know that You are a faithful God. I know that You have plans for me and for my children. Thank You that I can look back on my life and see Your provident hand upon it. I trust You with my future. Amen.

# H.O.M.E.S.C.H.O.O.L.

# H.O.M.E.S.C.H.O.O.L.

I am a "words" girl. I love to read and I love to write. I appreciate acronyms and I absolutely adore alliteration (see what I did there?). When the Established ministry was just starting up, I created an acronym for the word HOMESCHOOL:

### H = Home
Our home should be a place of rest, love, nurturing, teaching, and family. Our home should be a place of constant learning and where we feel most comfortable.

### O = Obedience
As parents, we obey Christ's commands as we teach our children to honor and obey the Lord and others in authority over them.

### M = Ministry
Homeschooling means ministering to our children's hearts and allowing the Lord to minster to ours.

### E = Experiences
When we homeschool, our children get experiences that others might not. Through each experience, we are able to educate.

### S = Skills
We are constantly teaching our children life-long skills. The Lord teaches us all spiritual lessons (not just reading, writing, and arithmetic).

## C = Create & Cultivate

In our homes, we can create and cultivate a close knit, loving environment and teachable spirits within our children.

## H = Hearts for Him

We want our children to have hearts for the Lord. That is our end goal. We can model a close relationship with Christ for our kids, in hopes that a relationship with Him will be the desire of their hearts as well.

## O = Observe

When we are with our children throughout the day, we are able to observe them. We can see strengths and weaknesses, and we can teach and train them where most needed.

## O = Opportunities

Our homeschooled children have many unique opportunities. Not only do we have flexibility in our schedules, but we can move as slowly or as quickly as needed. We can choose to double up the work on Thursday in order to take Friday off. We can even school in the car or in the doctor's office. We also have more "together time" and can enjoy more family meals together.

## L = Love for Learning

As homeschoolers, we want to instill within our students a love for learning. While learning isn't always fun (I'm thinking about algebra here!), we can play and laugh and take breaks when needed, so that our children don't get burnt out.

I think that this acronym sums up much of what we can do

when we teach our kids from home. The possibilities are endless! I can honestly say that I love learning alongside my children. I remember being pretty stressed out toward the end of our first year of homeschooling when it came time for state testing. One of my dearest friends (and a precious mentor) spoke encouragement to me during that time. I will never forget her telling me, "Kristi! One test is not a measure of what you have taught, or of what the boys have learned this year." What a weight lifted. Let's remember that our kids are learning things that are much more valuable than the Pythagorean Theorem. As they're being taught, the Lord is also teaching us many spiritual lessons. Let's give Him full reign in our hearts and in our homes!

# HEAR MY PRAYER:

Lord, I give You my heart. Teach me as I teach my children. Thank You for the blessing of not only having children to raise, but for the gift of being able to homeschool them. Help me to soak it all in, as time passes by so quickly. Help me to learn all of the lessons You desire to teach me. You are the Potter and I am the clay. Mold me. Make me into the parent and teacher You want me to be. Thank You for the opportunities and for the experiences we have shared as a family. Rule and reign in us, Lord. Amen.

# ON A MISSION

# ON A MISSION

When we were first getting the Established ministry up and running, we were blessed to have several "seasoned" homeschool moms come and speak to our group. One of the mentor moms spoke to us about creating mission statements for our schools and families. She gave us several things to consider when writing up a mission statement. Maria encouraged us to: list our roles, prioritize our roles, and create an action statement. I came home and talked with my kids, and that year we wrote out our family's mission statement. In hopes of encouraging you, I want to share it with you...

"We strive to honor and glorify God in word and deed. We seek to be a home that loves and serves Jesus. We desire to show Christ's love to one another and to others, both inside and outside of our home. We want to make Christ the center of our home and of our school. We hope to show love, respect, and responsibility at all times. We pray that we would be a family: used by God, consecrated to Him, and set apart in this world. We pray that our home would be a place where everyone feels loved, cherished, nurtured, and respected. Our home shall be a place of truth and trust, a place of learning and character training, and a place full of grace and growth."

Having a mission statement and posting it up in a central location will help to keep a clear focus. When you have a rough day and you feel like giving up, reading and remembering your long-term goals and your "why" will encourage you to stay the course. Through Christ's strength (and His strength alone) we are able to accomplish our goals.

Creating a mission statement also stirs in us an intentionality: in our parenting and in our schooling. If we are deliberate we will reap the benefits, we will see the fruit, and we will enjoy the spiritual rewards!

# HEAR MY PRAYER:

Lord, You are so faithful. I want to keep You at the forefront in my life and in my home. God, as I parent my children, I ask You to strengthen me and to uphold me. Help me to teach with intentionality. Jesus, I am on a mission and I will not allow the enemy to gain ground. With You- nothing is impossible! Lord God, please give me the endurance I need to press on in this calling. Lord, may I never forget "why" I am homeschooling my kids. I am raising them for Your kingdom and for Your glory. Amen!

# TEACH THEM DILIGENTLY

# TEACH THEM DILIGENTLY

I was reminded of Deuteronomy 6 this morning as I was thinking about my duties as a homeschooling mom...

*"Hear, O Israel: The Lord our God, the Lord is one! You shall love the Lord your God with all your heart, with all your soul, and with all your strength. And these words which I command you today shall be in your heart. You shall teach them diligently to your children, and shall talk of them when you sit in your house, when you walk by the way, when you lie down, and when you rise up. You shall bind them as a sign on your hand, and they shall be as frontlets between your eyes. You shall write them on the door posts of your house and on your gates." (Deut. 6:4-9)*

After reading this passage for the umpteenth time, the Lord is solidifying (in my heart and in my mind) the importance of parenting my children according to His Word. I am to model a relationship with Christ for my children and I am called to diligently teach them God's Word. I have a deep love for Webster's American Dictionary of the English Language, so I am constantly consulting my copy. Webster defines "diligently" as: with steady application and care; with industry or assiduity; not carelessly; not negligently. I don't know about you, but I am guilty. I am sure to teach the three R's everyday but I am not always intentional about investing in my kids' souls. I'll admit that I often take "time" for granted.

Our children are always learning from us...but WHAT are they learning? Are they learning how to be frazzled, stressed, impatient or hurried? Or are they learning how to cultivate a deep relationship with the Lord? Mine are probably learning "E) All of the above." When we homeschool, we have the unique opportunity to be with our children a lot more than parents who don't teach inside their homes. We are the ones they spend the most time with and we are, without a doubt, their biggest influences. We can take the time to pray and worship in the mornings (because we aren't rushing out the door to get to school on time!), and we can pray with them each night. We can talk about the Lord throughout the day and we can incorporate Him into everything we do. We can nip many issues in the bud since we are present, home, and available. We can use the Bible to correct and discipline in a loving way. We can even allot a certain time each day for Bible reading and devotions. We can work on Scripture memory with our kids, thus sharpening our own swords as well.

As I truly meditate on the passage in Deuteronomy, a holy conviction hits. Could I be doing more? The answer to that question will always be a resounding yes. I often allow the enemy to leave me feeling defeated and discouraged, but I shouldn't do that. God's grace is sufficient for me and for you. He is faithful to work in and through us, and in and through our children, as we seek to diligently teach them about His goodness! What can you do today, to invest in your child's eternal future?

# HEAR MY PRAYER:

Lord God, You are so good. You are so worthy of our praise and adoration. Lord, help me to be a godly example for my children. I confess that I fail daily. Develop in me a diligent heart. My desire is to know You more, and to love You more. Jesus, work in me and grow me...so that I might constantly teach my children of Your goodness and faithfulness. You alone are God! Please supply all that I need, so that I might teach my children of Your great love for them. Lord, I give You my heart. All of it. Have Your way in me. Have Your way in my children. I invite You into our home, and I desire Your presence. Mold me, as I shape my children for Your kingdom. Amen.

MAY YOUR CUP
BUBBLETH
OVER

# MAY YOUR CUP BUBBLETH OVER

My daughter loves to pour soda from the can into a cup of ice. She is getting better at knowing when to stop and wait for the fizz to settle, but she used to pour too much and too fast. You know how it goes: the carbonation causes the liquid to quickly rise and even spill out over the top. This gives me a visual: when Christ lives in us, evidence of His presence should spill out of us. We should overflow, so to speak. We should "bubble over" because of His goodness. When my cup is empty, I need a "refill" because I cannot pour from an empty cup. When I am not filled with His Word, nothing "good" can come from me. I need to daily fill my cup so that I can be used by God, to fulfill my purpose(s) as a homeschool mom.

How can we fill our cups? We can wake up and make our Lord the first One we talk to. We can spend quiet moments with Him...in His Word, in prayer, in worship. My starting the day with Him seems to set the tone for our school day. When I am not in the Word first thing, it's pretty apparent in my attitude and in the overall feel of our home throughout the day. I lack patience when interacting with my kids. I am not as slow to anger. I speak too soon or lash out in anger and frustration.

When I have been filled by the Spirit, I can teach and parent with a gentler tone. I am more prone to dish out hugs and praises than I am to implement consequences and punishments! Different seasons of life mean that we have to figure out what works for us.

A few years back, I spent time with a friend who literally spends all day with the Lord. She reads, she writes, she journals, and posts Scripture up all around her. She is blessed to be able to stay home, but her kids are grown and out of the house. I left her house feeling slightly envious of all of that time she has. I know my day will come, but these days, I don't have hours of uninterrupted time with the Lord. You may have fifteen minutes or you may have 115 minutes. Whatever amount of time you have, invest it with the Lord. He is so faithful to multiply. Remember to fill your cup, so that it may bubbleth over to your "students!"

# HEAR MY PRAYER:

Jesus, I need You. You are my Portion every day. May You be my first thought every morning, and my last each night. Lord, I want Your Word to be what spills out of me. Cause Your Word to come alive each day, as I read what You have written to me. Give me a heart of worship and an attitude of gratitude. Fill me with the Holy Spirit and help me to walk in the Spirit, not the flesh. I surrender all to You. I ask that You fill me daily, and that my children see Your love through me. Lord God, please give my kids a fervent love for You, and a hunger for Your Word. As they grow, may they desire You above all else. Fill them up, Jesus, I pray. Cause their love for You to spill out into an empty world. Amen.

# LET GRACE ABOUND

# LET GRACE ABOUND

Our kids know us better than anyone else, don't they? They get the best of us, and worst of us. The good. The bad. The ugly. There are no pretenses with them. No hiding who we truly are. They keep us honest...and humble. I have messed up time and time again. I've lost count of how many times I have had to apologize to my kids.

One thing I have noticed over my years of parenting and homeschooling is that kids are extremely forgiving. Mine are quick to give me a hug and tell me how much they love me (which makes me cry harder if I am already emotional). *Romans 5:20b-21 tell us: "But where sin abounded, grace abounded much more, so that as sin reigned in death, even so grace might reign through righteousness to eternal life through Jesus Christ our Lord."* This passage is a reminder for me that my kids are not the only wretched, little sinners around. The Lord is so gracious to me, and yet, I often lack grace in my disciplining, correcting, and parenting.

I had a frustrating conversation with one of my kids right before church this morning. Then, about two minutes into worship, the Lord convicted me. I knew I needed to apologize for my part. As quickly as the conviction came, a well-known Scripture came to mind. I knew that the Lord was speaking to my weary heart. If I want to receive the Lord's forgiveness and grace, I must give it. My kids will either see me modeling grace, or they will have a skewed picture of who God is, and how He parents us. The Lord chastens those He loves and we are called to do the same. With love. With grace.

# HEAR MY PRAYER:

Oh Jesus, I am so thankful for Your grace and for Your long-suffering toward me. You are so patient. Holy Spirit, You convict but never condemn. Lord, You are the perfect Parent. Jesus, as I seek to honor You with my life, please equip me. Please work in me. May my lips speak life and love. Shut my mouth before evil before rolls off my tongue. Help me to respond to sin with grace. Thank You, that though I sin daily, Your grace abounds. Thank You for the promise of eternal life, for all who trust in You. I long for the day when I am in Your presence. No more sin...no more sorrow. Jesus, I love You. Amen.

# HE IS
# FAITHFUL

# HE IS FAITHFUL

Our oldest son is a high school senior and will graduate in just a few weeks. It is such a weird time for a parent...such a mix of emotions. My heart swells with pride one minute, and then it is in a puddle the next. As Christian parents, we want nothing more than for our children to have their own relationships with the Lord. We are constantly teaching them, and as they grow and mature, the Lord brings about growth in us as well.

When we first began homeschooling ten years ago, I just had two boys. One was headed into third grade and one was beginning Kindergarten. As a former elementary school teacher, I was excited to teach my own boys. We set up desks, had a calendar hanging on the wall, and we said the Pledge of Allegiance every morning. One year turned into two and before I knew it, I was homeschooling with a newborn, then a toddler...and so on.

Now that I have ten years under my belt, it's easy for me to look back and see how the Lord has carried us through. There have been many days when I have wanted to throw in the towel, yet somehow by the end of each year my kids have finished their workbooks and they've learned their expected grade level material. I don't take credit, because I know it is only by His grace that we have completed year after year.

When we are obedient to the Lord and when we heed His calling, He will surprise us with great gifts and rewards. He is always faithful, whether we obey and listen or not.

However, it's awesome to reap the benefits of obedience. I am constantly telling my kids that "obedience brings blessing" and "disobedience leads to consequences." The Lord is ever-faithul to remind me that the same is true in my life. I cannot preach what I am not practicing myself.

The Christian life is exciting, when we are willing to obey-no matter the cost. Homeschooling is a sacrifice. It's not easy to wear all of the hats all of the time! I encourage you to continue to ask for direction. Sometimes it's a lack of peace that reveals that we aren't in His will, or that He has a new plan for us and is about to move us.

# HEAR MY PRAYER:

Lord, You are always faithful. I am not. You are so patient and You are constantly revealing Yourself to those who seek You. As I make decisions for my children, be the Head. Lord, I want You to be at the very center and core of my family. My desire is to follow Your lead. Lord, more of You and less of me. Jesus, bind the enemy and don't allow fear or doubt to creep in, as I parent and teach my children. Lord, may I always remember Your past faithfulness and trust in Your future plans for my family. Amen.

# SIGNS OF
# SPRING

# SIGNS OF SPRING

Each year, I get as giddy as a child on Christmas Day as the bare, wintery branches on my peach tree begin to blossom. First, I see the little buds, and within a week there are bright pink bursts sprouting up everywhere. I rush out to take pictures, and I practically jump up and down with excitement as I think of all the ways we will enjoy "my" peaches (homemade peach ice cream and cobbler are at the top of the list)! You see, my peach tree has been growing for over ten years. It has been growing longer than some of my children have been alive. Yet, it cycles through the various stages each year, and some aren't as pretty as others. The bare brown branches are necessary. I know that God's handiwork is taking place underground and within...but I cannot see it. Sometimes it feels like it's taking f o r e v e r, but before I know it- the signs of spring are here! Gazing upon the blossoms through my kitchen window each morning brings joy and excitement, because I know that there will soon be fruit to yield. It will be ripe for harvest in a few short months, and we will get to enjoy the bounty.

Isn't our Christian walk a lot like a tree? The Lord is always using my peach tree to minister to me, to teach me, to prune and refine me. There are some long and dark seasons. There are times when we can't see what the Lord is doing and we are left to trust that there will one day be "fruit." Our "branches" may seem bare, and we may even feel like we are not bearing much "fruit." Then, one day (or week or year) a bud appears and soon, a blossom. We begin to see the signs of the work done within. There are times of rejoicing in all that He has done. There are seasons of pure joy- as we delight in the produce of the growth. There are times of bounty. Whatever season you are in, let Him speak to you and minister to your heart.

Homeschooling can be much the same. Not every moment is pretty. Not every day is fun and/or adventurous. We may have seasons where we feel we are simply surviving (not thriving). When we are trying to teach our child a concept that he just can't seem to grasp, we need to look ahead and know that one day it will just click. When we are dealing with the same behavior issue(s) for months on end, we need to trust that, ultimately, there will be fruit. We shall continue to water "the trees" with the Living Water and we shall continue to feed them the Bread of Life. We shall always give them Son-light, knowing that our labor is not in vain. Whether our current homeschooling season is that of winter or of spring, we must trust and believe that the Lord is at work and look for the signs of spring!

# HEAR MY PRAYER:

Creator God, You are so good to us. Thank You for all of the unseen things You do. You are constantly at work in me and in my children. Even when I don't immediately see the fruit, I trust that You are moving and working. You are faithful. Help me, Lord, to have a godly patience and endurance as I wait for the ripening. Lord, have Your way in my children. Prune us, Lord, so that we might bear much fruit for Your kingdom. Amen.

# THE HARVEST

# THE HARVEST

When I think about October....it's "harvest" that comes to mind.

*"While the earth remains,*
*Seedtime and harvest,*
*Cold and heat,*
*Winter and summer,*
*And day and night*
*Shall not cease."*
*(Gen. 8:22)*

*"You have multiplied the nation and increased its joy; They rejoice before You according to the joy of harvest, As men rejoice when they divide the spoil." (Is. 9:3)*

*"A time to plant, and a time to pluck what is planted...." (Ecc. 3:2b)*

*"And let us not grow weary while doing good, for in due sesaon we shall reap if we do not lose heart..."*
*(Gal. 6:9)*

When I read these passages, I am reminded that putting in the work- to prepare for the harvest- is often NOT easy! As a matter of fact, many days and seasons are hard, trying, and even downright discouraging. But isn't the harvest so very worth it? The farmer wouldn't do it if it wasn't! The same is true for us. We wouldn't homeschool if we didn't have long term, eternal "goals." We know we are called to this, and we press on...through the planting, the watering, the waiting.

When I think of my children as my harvest, I can be encouraged on those harder days. I can open God's Word and be comforted by His promises. I can look to Him as my Hope, my Sustainer, and my Refuge. On those tough days, we need to remember why we are homeschooling. We collectively desire to instruct our children biblically and we are hoping to train them up in His ways. We are hoping to be the primary influence(s) in our kids' lives, and we want them to imitate us as we imitate Christ. Of course, we are going to fall short...and we are going to mess up. It's part of this parenting gig- no matter how much we desire to honor the Lord.

However, even in our flaws and failures...our kids should be able to see our hearts. We should be able to apologize to them when we are not representing Christ well. After all, they're not the only ones being harvested. Thank God...that He is continuously working ON us and that He is faithful to complete that which He has begun IN us! Here's to a bountiful harvest this school year!!

# HEAR MY PRAYER:

God, You are Sustainer. You are Provider. You are constantly at work in us, preparing us to yield a harvest. As I seek You, as I dive into Your Word, as I commune and dialogue with You, prune me. Please remove any rotten fruit and trim away anything in me that is not of You. Work in my children and in our home. Lord, it is with excitement that I look forward to the reaping. As I water these little "seeds" that You have given me, may You do a mighty work as You grow and weed us. Amen.

PURPOSES
FULFILLED

# PURPOSES FULFILLED

*"May He give you what your heart desires and fulfill your whole purpose." (Psalm 20:4, CSB)*

Last week, I was reading through the psalms and I came to Psalm 20:4. I was struck by the fact that I have probably read this verse fifty times, and yet, it had never previously had such impact on me. I continued on and read the whole psalm and yet...I was drawn back to verse 4. I just sat...in awe...of the God who wrote the verse. I couldn't get over the fact that He cares so much about little 'ole me, that He would cause it to "pop" out at me in a new and profound way. What an incredible "word" to share with our children. Amen?!

As we spend our days homeschooling our children, thus fulfilling part of our purpose on this earth- we can read this verse and be reminded of His goodness, His plans, His will, and His desires for us. We know, as believers in Christ, that the desires of our hearts will line up with His, when we are seeking Him and walking closely with Him. Psalm 20:4 is an amazing verse for us to share with our children- to remind them that, through it all, the good days and the tough ones our God wants to give us the desires of our hearts. He wants to fulfill His WHOLE purpose in their lives.

I am so thankful that He promises to finish what He started... and I am beyond grateful that He is not done with me yet. It is my prayer, for my family and for yours, that we would honor Him with our lives. That we would seek Him as we live out our callings, and that He would give us the desires of our hearts (which are actually His desires for us)! I pray you are blessed today, and that you can walk in the power, strength, and victory that come only from Jesus!

# HEAR MY PRAYER:

Lord, it is my desire that You would work in me and that I would fulfill my God-given purposes as a parent and a teacher. I seek to live for You, to honor You, and to lead and teach in a way that honors You. Lord, may my children walk in all that You have for them. May they desire to please You, to obey Your Holy Word, and to serve You wholeheartedly. Use our family. May we be Your willing servants. Amen.

# WORD SEARCH

# WORD SEARCH

For many of us, January means a fresh start. A clean slate. A chance to begin anew. A few years back, my best friend mentioned the idea of asking the Lord for a "word" for each year. I began to ask Him for my word and I would wait with expectation. My God is so faithful, and He has never left me hanging! He has always provided words for me. As 2017 came to a close, I began asking Him for my 2018 word. It wasn't until New Year's Day that He spoke clearly to my heart: quiet. As soon as He put the word on my heart, I knew. This word would be a challenge for me, as I am not naturally quiet.

I knew right away that the word meant more than just being quiet. Rather, it meant quieting my heart before the Lord, quieting my mouth (being slow to speak, or not speaking at all), quieting my life a bit (finding balance in my schedule), using a quieter tone when talking to my children, and quieting my mind (by seeking Him first and not allowing myself to be distracted). I will admit that though I knew this was to be "my word" for the year, I wasn't all that thrilled at first.

Later, other words that seemed better to me came to mind. Isn't it just like our God, though, to know what we NEED? He didn't give me a word that was comfortable for me. He gave me a word that would cause me to NEED Him. A word that would maybe even make me squirm a bit. Nonetheless, it's a much needed one for me.

As I was reading this morning, I came to *Matthew 17:5, which* says: *"This is My beloved Son, with whom I am well pleased. Listen to Him!"* Instantly, I was reminded that I cannot listen to someone if I am not quiet. Oh, how sweet and good and kind He is to me...to confirm what He has put on my heart.

I realize the idea of asking for a word, or even choosing one for yourself, may not be for everyone. I like to look at it as a different way of approaching a new year. I'm not big into resolutions!

Maybe the Lord does have a word for you. My prayer for each of you is that you would have a renewed strength and zeal to finish the school year strong. What a privilege we have been given: the ability and freedom to homeschool our kids! May we see it as such. May we invest in our kids. May we be quiet enough to hear them. May we truly listen to them. May we seek the Lord as we raise these arrows for His kingdom and teach them according to His Word. Happy New Year!

# HEAR MY PRAYER:

Jesus, Thank You for speaking to my heart. Thank You for moving in my life. Thank You for using me, even though I am a sinner in need of a Savior. Lord, please quiet my heart before You. I want to receive all that You have for me. Lord, drown out the background noise so that I might listen. I want to hear You. I want to know You. Remove worldly distractions, so that I can sit in Your presence and draw from Your Word. Thank You for the privilege I have to homeschool my children. Thank You that I am free to teach my kids at home. Please continue to reveal Yourself to me. Amen.

HANDS
HELD HIGH

# HANDS HELD HIGH

*Then Amalek came and fought with Israel at Rephidim. So Moses said to Joshua, "Choose for us men, and go out and fight with Amalek. Tomorrow I will stand on the top of the hill with the staff of God in my hand." So Joshua did as Moses told him, and fought with Amalek, while Moses, Aaron, and Hur went up to the top of the hill. Whenever Moses held up his hand, Israel prevailed, and whenever he lowered his hand, Amalek prevailed. But Moses' hands grew weary, so they took a stone and put it under him, and he sat on it, while Aaron and Hur help up his hands, one on one side, and the other on the other side. So his hands were steady until the going down of the sun. And Joshua overwhelmed Amalek and his people with the sword.*

*Then the LORD said to Moses, "Write this as a memorial in a book and recite it in the ears of Joshua, that I will utterly blot out the memory of Amalek from under heaven." And Moses built an altar and called the name of it, "The LORD Is My Banner, saying, "A hand upon the throne of the LORD! The LORD will have war with Amalek from generation to generation."*

*(Exodus 17:8-16)*

When I read this passage several years back, something became very profound to me. When Moses grew weary, two of his closest friends came alongside him and held up his hands. He had one "helper" on either side of him, literally holding his hands up so that the Israelites would continue to prevail in battle. When he had grew weary and didn't have the energy to hold his own hands up any longer, they were right there...

ready to do what was needed to win the battle. Aaron and Hur steadied Moses. Can you imagine how this would have encouraged his heart?

Friends, isn't life like this? We tend to grow weary from the day in, day out "battles" we face. We can start to lose strength and we often lack the perseverance that these battles require of us. Our enemy begins defeating us. What are we to do? First, what we need is time alone with Jesus. We need to daily put on our armor (Eph. 6:10-18), but we also need friends. We need that "community" that we were created for. We need others to hold us up when we are tired, weary, and want to give up.

Our enemy seeks to isolate us. He wants us to feel alone in our battles, and he wants us to feel hopeless, desperate, and defeated. As he plants seeds of doubt, our strength is sapped. His lies weaken our resolve. We have to be intentional when it comes to battling him.

I find that a certain peace comes when I share my struggle, and when I reach out for prayer or encouragement. We find that we are actually not alone when we ask our friends to hold us up. When we are authentic and transparent in our relationships, we can receive prayer and the Lord can begin to do a work within us.

Today, I encourage you to reach out to a friend. Send a text, pick up the phone, or surprise her with a coffee. If you are the friend that needs your arms held up, don't hesitate to ask for prayer from those closest to you. The enemy can't "win" when we bring our struggles/sins/ needs/burdens into the light...and there is such power in prayer! If you need prayer, please don't hesitate to email me at: kmenashewrites@gmail.com. I vow to lift you up!

*"A friend loves at all times and a brother is born for adversity."* *(Proverbs 17:17)*

Be blessed and encouraged today, parents. I am praying for you!

# HEAR MY PRAYER:

Jesus, Thank You for not only being my heavenly Father, but also my friend. Thank You that I have complete access to You at all times. Lord, thank You for creating me for community. Thank You for godly friends that You have brought into my life, and that I can reach out during times of struggle and trials. Lord, may You be the first One that I run to with my needs. Please give me wisdom on when to ask for help and for prayer from like-minded friends. God, please provide godly friends for my children. Surround them with Your angels and please put a hedge of protection around them. Amen.

# A DIFFERENT VIEW

# A DIFFERENT VIEW

The other day we visited the Safari Park in San Diego. We walked to the gorilla exhibit, excited to watch the fascinating creatures. I stood smack dab in the middle of the exhibit... only there was nothing to see. I started to feel disappointed, but a few minutes went by and we saw one gorilla come out. I watched him for a minute, but he didn't do much. I looked off to the side of the exhibit, and I could see my husband in the distance, waving me his direction. I walked toward him, saw him pointing down, and wouldn't you know it? From his vantage point, about six more gorillas could be seen, including a baby and a toddler.

All of the gorilla action was happening in a location that couldn't be seen from the "front and center" spot. Instead, my husband had found a more obscure spot to stand, where he could peek down into the ditch within their habitat. As we stood there, watching those incredible creatures- playing, chasing and swatting each other, and even circling their mother, I thought about God's children. About how often we stand "front and center" when God has a different view for us. He calls us to a better location. To a spot we wouldn't see if we just stood at the front of the exhibit on our own.

From the hidden location, I looked down to the front of the exhibit, where a large group had gathered. They stood there... watching one gorilla, looking around for more. 'If they only knew the view we are beholding!' I thought. How often am I satisfied with the one gorilla, who's not doing much? Yet my

God wants so much more for me. He invites me over, and He points me toward the real show. Often times, He calls us to more so that He might teach us or reveal areas where we need change. Sometimes, it's for our enjoyment or simply to encourage our hearts.

In my devotional this morning, I read: "We're all too satisfied. We're all too satisfied with who we are, where we are, and what we're doing. We're satisfied with a little bit of biblical literacy. We're satisfied with occasional moments of ministry. We're satisfied with faithful attendance at the weekend services of our churches. We're satisfied with quick morning devotions. But here's what you and I need to remember: we serve a dissatisfied Redeemer. He knows we still need the transforming work of His powerful grace!"

My desire is to be looking up...to see Him waving me over. To be open to what He has for me. To be dissatisfied with the mediocre view, so that I might see ALL that He has for me. As I minister to my husband, as I teach my children, as I serve others, or even just go about my mundane duties and tasks, may I search for the view He has for me. May I learn as I teach. May I grow as He teaches me. May I be dissatisfied until I am seeing things from His vantage point. Praying the same for you!

# HEAR MY PRAYER:

Lord God, I want to see things as You do. Help me to align myself with Your will and Your plans. Cause me to view things from a heavenly perspective. Lord, I want to be exactly where You want me and to be nowhere else. God, please give my children the desire to follow You. Use me to guide them and lead them down the path to everlasting life. Lord God, I don't want to be satisfied with mediocre. I long for the majestic views You offer me. Draw near to me, as I draw near to You. Amen.

# WHAT REALLY
# MATTERS

# WHAT REALLY MATTERS

*"For what profit is it to a man if he gains the whole world, and loses his own soul? Or what will a man give in exchange for his soul?" (Matthew 16:26)*...has been a recurring verse for me over the last few months. I have heard it used in several different capacities, and the Lord keeps impressing it upon my heart in quiet moments as well. While I have my own personal convictions regarding this verse, my heart today is to encourage you, the homeschooling parent, to keep training your children up in the ways of the Lord.

If our children get the highest test scores, are accepted into Ivy League schools, become neurosurgeons, or even make millions of dollars, but they do not love and serve Jesus, none of those other things matter! As much as we want our children to "succeed" in life and in this world, what matters most is the capturing of their hearts and the surrendering of their wills. Their job titles or college degrees means nothing if they aren't headed to heaven.

I have been around long enough to observe many Christian families, and some of the strongest families I know currently have prodigals. I write this to encourage and never to make a parent feel badly about what they have or have not done. We can teach godly characteristics and we must model them for our children, but ultimately our children will go on to decide for themselves whether or not they want to walk with God. It comes down to the position of their hearts.

Through my homeschooling years, I have learned that some of the most important lessons aren't taught in textbooks. Don't get me wrong- my family uses them and my kids complete them each year. However, I have learned that state test scores don't matter as much as the state of my children's hearts. I do want them to grow up to be responsible adults, respectable citizens, and diligent workers. There's something I want more than all of that, though. My desire is for my children to grow in the grace and knowledge of the Lord, to use the gifts and talents He has given them, and to be consecrated unto Him.

Each day, I mess up. Each day, they mess up. We are constantly learning to give and receive grace. We often fail and have to apologize. Sadly, I don't always point them to Jesus right off the bat. We get angry. We sin. We make mistakes and have to ask for forgiveness. Thankfully, at the end of the day, my children know my heart's desire is to spend eternity with them. They also know that it is their decision as to where they choose to spend eternity. We are learning together. We are growing and maturing. Sometimes it's not as fast as I'd like, but we are so grateful that we serve a patient God.

Keep feeding the Word of God to your kiddos. Keep praying as a family and thanking Him as He answers. Keep apologizing when you mess up. Keep telling your kids how much you love them and how much MORE God does. Keep your eyes on Jesus- whether you're on top of the mountain or deep in a valley- and remember that we all have the same desire for our kids. We want their "profit" to be heaven...with us...for eternity!

# HEAR MY PRAYER:

Jesus, Thank You for dying on the cross. Thank You for rising from the dead. Thank You for offering us eternal life with You. Lord, there is nothing I want more than for my children to be in heaven with me and with You. The enemy hates me and he hates my children, but greater is He who is in me than he who is in the world. Lord, please work in my children, so that their hearts become soft to the things of You. Put a hedge of protection around them. May they seek You. May they know You. May they love You more than anything or anyone else. Lord, constantly work in me so that my children can imitate me as I imitate You. You are so worthy. Amen.

# LOVE WELL

# LOVE WELL

A while back, I was listening to a sermon and the pastor stated that everyday he asks the Lord, "What would You have me do today?" He said that usually the Lord gives him one or two things to do. Sometimes it's as simple as: "Call your son and take him to lunch," while other days the tasks are bigger. He has passed up events with bigwigs, to sometimes do tasks that feel/seem less important. However, those jobs are exactly what the Lord wants from him and they are the more important thing.

Listening to this caused me to think, and to consider asking the Lord this very question. I can't say that I ask it everyday, but usually when I do, it's not a task that sounds difficult. Most of the time, the Lord's response to my heart is for me to love my children well. That may not seem like a tough thing to do, but when we homeschool our children- they are with us ALL. THE. TIME. 24/7! Because they are with me all the time, my children can get on my nerves and wear me down. (Anyone feel me?) I lose patience, I feel defeated, I lack grace, and the list goes on. When this happens, I remind myself of the truths in His Word: Children are GIFTS from God. They are arrows in the hands of warriors. They're our heritage. We love because He first loved us, and we are to train them up in the way they should go. We should be able to say, as Paul did, "Imitate me as I imitate Christ."

Loving our children doesn't have to mean extravagance. For me, it can mean reading an extra chapter aloud to them (mine love that!), making their favorite lunch, giving them an unexpected hug, complimenting them when they are working hard, writing them a little note to find, playing a family game all together, using a gentle tone, and even giving grace when I don't feel like it.

How can you love your children well today? What is He asking you to do in order to glorify and honor him?

Keep fighting the good fight, friends. We have been given a BIG responsibility- not only as parents, but homeschoolers. May we always view our task(s) as a privilege and feel honored that He chose us for our kiddos!

# HEAR MY PRAYER:

Oh Jesus, You are so good and Your love is perfect. My love fails daily. I desire to love like You do. I desire to love my family well. Lord, create a clean heart in me. Renew my spirit when I am weary and battle worn. God, reveal to me what You would have me do this day to show love to my family and to others. Abba, please cause me to be quick to listen for Your prompting. Tune my heart to hear Your voice and steer me toward obedience. Work in me so that I might be willing to do whatever You ask of me. Help me to surrender my motives and expectations to heed Your call. Lord, please move in my life. May my children see You at work in me. Amen.

# THE MOST
# IMPORTANT WORK

# THE MOST IMPORTANT WORK

I don't know about you, but the Lord uses my kids to teach me about Himself more than anything or anyone else. He constantly has personal lessons for me to learn...about His grace. About His mercy. About His agape love. Never condemning (that's the enemy's job), but always convicting. I become aware of how very short I fall. Yet, somehow after there is conviction, there is also a gentle ministering to my heart and an encouragement for my soul.

A certain quote I once heard keeps coming to mind lately: "Children are not a distraction from more important work. They are the most important work." I feel this statement packs an even bigger punch for us as homeschoolers. See, our children are always with us. Like... always! There are times we long for a break, or for just a few moments to ourselves and I don't think that is a bad thing. In fact, I think it is needed. What I am referring to is a knowing- of when to take that time away, and when to let our children "come" to us. That might sound strange, considering they are always with us. Let me explain...

The Lord recently spoke to my heart and He revealed a few areas in my life where I was viewing my children as interruptions. Ouch. He spoke these things to me on a morning after an extremely busy day. I had been running from place to place. Things felt hectic, and as I met with a friend, my kids kept interrupting me. "I'm thirsty." "I need to go potty." "When are we leaving?" I would like to tell you that my responses were full of grace and patience- but they were not. I was annoyed. I'll leave out most of the details, but imagine rolling eyes, hastily grabbing a hand and power walking to the restroom while "shushing" repeatedly. Fast forward to the next morning...with Bible open and pen in hand...praying and journaling...

DO NOT HINDER YOUR CHILDREN IN COMING TO YOU. Clear as day (and in all caps!), this is what the Lord laid on me. If I could insert an emoji here, it would be the one with the big, wide eyes! What followed that exhortation was: Even during your quiet time, involve them and ask them "Did you know?" questions. Use every opportunity to teach them. I understand that these are my personal convictions and that things are going to look differently in each home. We pour so much into our kids, as they are our main ministry (aside from marriage). This is an encouragement to get alone with the Lord and to seek Him. Read, pray, listen, write. We cannot pour from an empty cup.

As I sat down to write this, I was able to put into practice what the Lord had shown me. My six-year-old rose very early, then came and sat on my lap and began smothering me in kisses. I had to laugh. Being a mom is the most important role I'll ever play. Life isn't a dress rehearsal. I don't have these days to do over again. I won't get these years back. May I always be mindful that as I am teaching them, He is teaching me. I pray the same for you.

# HEAR MY PRAYER:

Jesus, Thank You that You never slumber or sleep. Thank You that I can come boldly and confidently to You at any time. Thank You for loving me, and for desiring a relationship with me. Thank You that You always want me to be close to You. Lord, grow me as a mom and a teacher. I want my children to always feel they can come to me, just as I do with You. I confess that I have considered my children "interruptions" before, and I am sorry, God. Thank You, Lord, for the ministry of motherhood. May I be a tangible representation of You, and may I honor You in word and deed as I raise my children up for Your kingdom. Amen.

# LET HIM LEAD

# LET HIM LEAD

I taught my oldest son at home for eight years, and then the Lord began to speak to my husband about our son finishing out his last two years of high school at a Christian school. I'll admit that I was not on board. I had grown used to our flexible schedule. I acted selfishly until a good friend encouraged me to attend an orientation at the school. Before my husband, son, and I went, I prayed and prayed that the Lord would bring clarity on orientation day.

From the moment we set foot on the campus, I could feel Him working on my heart. By the time we left that day, God had made it clear that Bryson's attending school was His plan. Though I felt a certainty, I struggled, knowing that in a few short days, life as we knew it would be ending. It took us some time to get used to the new schedule. We missed our boy. He auditioned for the school musical during the second week of school. Things felt odd as we quickly went from always being together to him being gone for up to sixteen hours each day (due to rehearsals and performances).

Even though it was different, and parts of it were hard, we knew it was "right." I share this with you, to encourage you. Continue praying and ask the Lord where He wants you and your children. Be open to Him switching things up, especially when you least expect it. I used to think that what we do for one child, we must do for all. The longer that I am a parent, and the more I see the different needs, strengths, weaknesses, and struggles of my children, the more I realize that is just not true.

Meeting the needs of each of my children won't be easy. Their stories won't look the same. We may never send our others to school, or we may.

The Lord may call me to homeschool every year- until my youngest graduates in 2031 (please, Lord- take us Home before then!) or He may have a different plan. I want to follow His leading, and I can only do that if I am in the Word and dialoguing with Him consistently. Stay in communion with Him! Stay connected to the Vine! Try not to make your own plans but listen for His prompting. Wait for Him to lead and guide! He is always faithful.

# HEAR MY PRAYER:

Lord, You are such a personal God. You long for me to dialogue with You and You long to reveal Yourself to Your people. As I seek Your direction for my kids, Lord, please guide and impart wisdom. Please bring clarity, so that I may walk in Your will. Lord, please lead me and my family. We want to follow You. I trust in Your perfect timing. Help me to be patient as I wait upon You. Amen.

CONFIDENCE
& GRACE

# CONFIDENCE & GRACE

One thing we realize very quickly is that everyone has an opinion regarding homeschooling. It took me several years to learn how to graciously respond to people's comments and questions. As each year passes, homeschooling seems to become more widely accepted, though there are still naysayers.

At the end of the day, we as parents all want what's best for our children. I believe that our schooling choices are just that: ours. We won't all choose the same paths. When we remember that we all love our children and that we are going to parent, discipline, and school differently, grace and understanding exist.

If you're experiencing opposition of any sort, pray that the Lord would give you His words to speak, or that He will hold your tongue. Ask for wisdom on how to reply and respond. Have a little "tool belt" full of standard answers for those broader questions. Can your children still attend college? What about prom? Don't they miss their friends? Do your kids wear their pajamas all day? How do you socialize them? These are all questions I've been repeatedly asked. I'm sure you've gotten the same.

I have been insecure for as long as I can remember, but I've had to adopt the "fake it til you make it" philosophy with regards to homeschooling. I cannot deny that it was the Lord who called my family to this. Therefore, I can answer these questions with certainty. Over the years, He has given me a true confidence-knowing that I am in His will.

As I write this, we have just finished up our tenth year. I know the Lord calls some families to homeschool for one year while others have twenty plus under their belts. My family will continue to pray and seek Him and as long as there is a peace, we will trust that this is where He wants us.

The world is growing increasingly dark and I am thankful that I can be the primary influence in my children's lives. If He has called you to teach your children in your home, you can walk confidently in all that He has for you and your kids. Respond with grace, patience, and love. You just never know how He will use you, and it's possible you'll be the very example and witness He will use to call someone else to homeschool as well.

# HEAR MY PRAYER:

Father, You are gracious. You are patient. You are kind. Lord, I want to be slow to speak and quick to listen. I want to respond in grace. Jesus, please give me Your words to speak...always. I want to represent You well. I want others to see me shining, so that they praise You! May the words of my mouth be pleasing to You, God. Hold my tongue when I don't have anything nice to say. Use me as a vessel for Your Kindgom's cause. Amen.

# STRENGTH ON THE
# BATTLEFIELD

# STRENGTH ON THE BATTLEFIELD

I love the Lord's timing and how when He wants us to hear (really HEAR Him), He will make sure that we are lovingly bombarded with reoccurring messages (themes, verses, etc.) Lately, He has really been drilling into me that I need to stop, listen, and obey. I can't hear from Him if I am not obeying. If I want to be His vessel, I must first be walking in obedience. In my current Bible study, we spent some time reading through Genesis– when God called Abraham to "get up and go." We don't read that Abraham hesitated, but that he listened and obeyed. He didn't delay, even when God was asking him to do BIG and hard things. Leave his land? Leave his family? And later to even be willing to sacrifice the son he had waited years for? Because Abraham obeyed, he was blessed greatly by God. His obedience was accounted to him as righteousness!

Today, I was reading to my boys from Joshua 10 and my heart was so encouraged! Long story short: Joshua's enemies (five kings) tried to attack him and the Israelites at Gibeon. The men of Gibeon were fearful and freaked out a bit, but the Lord said to Joshua: *"Do not be afraid of them, for I have handed them over to you. Not one of them will be able to stand against you."* With the Lord as their Commander, Joshua and his armies defeated them, and they fled. Joshua spoke to the Lord in the presence of Israel, telling the sun to stand still. In verse 14, we read: *"There has been no day like it before or since, when the Lord listened to a man, because the Lord fought for Israel."* Wow! I don't know about you, but this is a real faith-builder for me! The rest of chapter ten is amazing (see for yourself!), because we continue to read of how Joshua defeated every last one of them. Joshua was able to say to his men the very thing that the Lord spoke to him: *"Do not be afraid or discouraged. Be strong and courageous, for the Lord will do this to all the enemies you fight."*

As we face potential threats against homeschooling, we are faced with two options: run at our enemy boldly and courageously or shrink back in fear and do nothing. I love the example of Abraham, who immediately listened to the Lord and obeyed Him, and of Joshua, who boldly took his men into battle knowing the Lord had already handed his enemies over to him, is also extremely encouraging. Joshua reassured his men with the very words God had spoken to him. I want to do that!

As believers and homeschoolers, we are passionate about defending our rights and freedoms. Now is our time to listen to the Lord and to obey Him. Now is the time to run at the enemy, not from him, knowing our God (our Battle Fighter) fights for us. If He could cause life to grow in Sarah's womb after years of barrenness, provide a ram in a thicket as a sacrifice, and cause the sun to stand still, shouldn't we have faith that He can defend us, and defeat our enemy, today?! Parents, I encourage you to rise up when "homeschooling" is threatened. Pray boldly! We have victory in the One who fights on our behalf!

# HEAR MY PRAYER:

God, You are my Battle Fighter. I can rest in You and there is no reason for me to fear or to doubt. You can do anything and Your Word says that nothing is too hard for You. Lord, cause me to stand for freedom and for righteousness. God, please bring clarity when there are times I need to stand strong and fight. Lord, I know I will experience victory when I am following You. You have given me all that I need to battle the enemy. May I use my sword as I trust in Your powerful name. My hope is in You alone! Amen.

# DOWN HOMESCHOOL ROAD

# DOWN HOMESCHOOL ROAD

Before I began homeschooling, I started talking to all of my friends who were already walking down Homeschool Road. I asked what curricula they used; I learned what they loved and what they didn't. I researched my options and spent lots of time praying and discovering this new (to me) world.

At first, it was all very overwhelming to me. It seemed there were innumerable choices for everything from curriculum options to private satellite programs, extracurricular classes, sports leagues, conventions, and online classes. Many friends encouraged me by sharing what worked for them. I knew that once we started, it would take some time to figure out what worked for my family.

Looking back, our beginning years mimicked a typical classroom setting. My kids sat in desks and we pledged to the flag. I would give my "students" recess and lunch breaks. (I even made them call me "Mrs. Menashe." Just kidding!) Through the years, we all gravitated to the kitchen table and the desks were eventually sold. I had to learn that we all do things differently, and that there is beauty in that.

I love listening to speakers and seasoned homeschool moms share experiences, ideas, and schedules. I continue to glean from others and it's always refreshing to hear about how other homes are run.

In the beginning, I remember feeling fearful that I was going to mess up my kids by homeschooling them. Over the years I have come to the conclusion that as long as I am following the Lord, I have nothing to fear. That is not to say that my children won't face challenges, that I won't disappoint them at times, or that I don't struggle with pleasing people occasionally. My children may graduate from high school not fully knowing how to diagram sentences and they may not remember the difference between meiosis and mitosis, but they will know that their parents prayed over the decision to homeschool them. They'll know we desire for them to love the Lord above all else. They will know our hopes, our dreams, and our expectations. They will know what we believe about God and His Word, and Lord-willing, they will want a deep relationship with Him for themselves.

When we are headed down Homeschool Road, we need to remember to stay in our own lane. Do that which the Lord calls YOU to. Try not to pick apart those who are schooling and parenting differently than you. I always say that if there was some magic formula we could follow that guaranteed our kids wouldn't make mistakes and that they'd always love Jesus and never walk away from Him, we would all be doing that. Though we don't have a magic formula, we have His powerful Word.

Be the friend and encourager we all so desperately need. Give godly counsel when asked. Stay away from offering unsolicited advice. Pray WITH others when their roads are rocky. Ask for prayer when you hit a hurdle. Though we are each in our own lanes, we are on the road together!

# HEAR MY PRAYER:

Lord God, Thank You for calling me to homeschool my children. Thank You for revealing to me the path that You desire for my family. Lord, as I walk this road, please guide me and my children. I want You to steer us, Lord. As we hit bumps and hurdles, may we press harder into You. Don't let me veer off, Lord. Keep me and my kids on the path that leads to everlasting life. Holy Spirit, bring to mind a friend who needs encouraging. Use me to be a voice of truth, life, and love today. Amen.

Kristi and her husband, Josh, live in Southern California with their four children. Kristi and Josh have been married for twenty-three years and have attended Calvary Chapel Chino Hills for twenty years. Kristi and her family love traveling and enjoying outdoor activities together. Kristi enjoys being part of CCCH's prayer team, mentoring women in the Sister2Sister program, and hosting Bible studies in her home. Kristi has homeschooled for ten years, and she is the founder of Established. She is an avid reader and has had a lifelong passion for writing.

**Email Kristi: kmenashewrites@gmail.com**
**Instagram: @k.menashe.writes**